SEVEN DEADLY SINS

PRIDE
ROZ KAVENEY and GRAHAM HIGGINS
ENVY
TYM MANLEY and HUNT EMERSON
SLOTH
NEIL GAIMAN and BRYAN TALBOT
GLUTTONY
DAVE GIBBONS and LEW STRINGER
GREED
MARK RODGERS and STEVE GIBSON
ANGER
DAVY FRANCIS and JEREMY BANKS
LUST
ALAN MOORE and MIKE MATTHEWS

KNOCKABOUT CRACK EDITIONS

PRIDE

ROZ KAVENEY and GRAHAM HIGGINS

PRIDE

A CLASSIC STRIP by GRAHAM HIGGINS © 1989

featuring AN EXQUISITE COMMENTARY by ROZ KAVENEY

THOUGH WHY WE WASTE OUR COMBINED ERUDITION ON THE LIKES OF YOU WE DON'T KNOW

HUW PREECE, A WALKING CATALOGUE OF MISERY : UNQUALIFIED, UNEMPLOYED AND **WELSH.**
HIS SATURDAY NIGHT COMPRISES: TWELVE PINTS OF **LAGER**, A LOUD **LEER** AT THE PUB **ENTERTAINMENT** — (BILL PROSSER AT THE ORGAN ACCOMPANYING DOLLY MADOC'S DANCE OF THE SEVEN THERMAL UNDERGARMENTS) — AN INFORMAL **BRAWL**, AND...

DAI PUGH Est.1956
PIE 'N' MASH
HOT SNACKS BEVERAGES
MASH 'N' PIE

...FISH FINGER AN' CHIPS OFF **DAI PUGH**. NICE AND **GREASY** TO GIVE YOUR **BELLY** SOMETHIN' TO GRIP **HOLD** OF...

OLD **YUKKY DAI**'S NEVER SHORT OF TRADE COME SAT'DY NIGHT.

There was once a poor fisherman, unhappy with his lot . . .

Of course, in the versions *you* will all know, this wonderful lecture on the perils of ambition ends up becoming a lot of misogynist nonsense. We, especially since I patiently explained the politics to Higgins, are above all that. This is not the shop to which you come for **The Story of the Fisherman and his Wife,** but a superior, purer version . . . Note how, in Mr Higgins's elegant rendition, the play of light and shade captures the rancid crunch of aged batter.

WHAT'S **PUKEY PUGH** GOT THAT I 'AVEN'T?

A **BUSINESS**, THAT'S WHAT. **WELL** I MAY NOT HAVE **NOTHIN'**...

BUT I GOT ME **PRIDE**!

...I GOT MESELF **TOGETHER**— BOUGHT AN EXPENSIVE **OVERCOAT** AND WENT AND **SWEET-TALKED** THE **BANK. BINGO**! I HAD MESELF A LITTLE **BUSINESS. EASY**, EH? SUDDENLY I WAS TAKING **MONEY HAND** OVER **BLIDDY FIST**...

I HAD SOMETHING T'BE **PROUD** OF. PROUD OF **MESELF**? YOU BET!

He caught a fish, and the fish was a magic fish, and in his hands it spoke to him, and it said 'Let me go, and I will give you your heart's desire.'

Ours is not a time for magic fish that speak: note the rare brilliance with which Mr Higgins and I have reduced the outmoded idea of magic to a mere soupcon, a food additive, if you like.

'TIS FRESH INNIT, YOUNG HUGH?

FRESH, GRANNY OWEN? FRESH? LOVELY BIT O'COD, LOVE. Y'WOULDN'T GET BETTER UP THE WEST END...

IN FACT, I THINK I'LL HAVE A BIT MESELF... THERE'S LOVELY!

HMM... WEST END, EH?

GET A LOAD OF THE GLITZ, EH? GALA OPENING OF MY KNIGHTSBRIDGE EATERIE. WHO'D HAVE THOUGHT IT? A LAD FROM THE VALLEYS MIXING IT WITH TV PERSONALITIES 'N' THAT. AND LISTEN, THIS MOB'LL PAY THROUGH THE NOSE FOR A BIT OF REAL FOOD. MORE MONEY 'N' SENSE, MOST OF 'EM.

LOOK AT 'EM. COMMON AS MUCK, MOST OF 'EM, GETTING BACK TO THEIR ROOTS. IT'LL COST 'EM, MIND. CLASS DON'T COME CHEAP.

YOU PAYIN' OR WHAT?

DAHLING, WHAT A HORRID LITTLE MAN!

SO AUTHENTIC, DAHLING, SO EARTHY, SO ETHNIC!

HOPE I DIE BEFORE I GET POOR

DON' I KNOW YOU? HARPO?

IT'S THE DISH THAT PUT THE QUEASY IN NOUVELLE CUISINE

THREE... NO FOUR THOUSAND PENN'ORTH OF CHIPS AND A SAVELOY

MAKE YOUR TINY MIND UP, FATSO.

And when he had his heart's desire, he was happy for a while, and then it seemed a slight thing to him. He went out again, and again he held the fish in his hands, and it said to him . . .

Here we see Higgins insisting on adding a lot of oh-so-piquant contemporary references, a veritable charivari or charabanc of caricatures, to what I had intended as a subtly stark bridge passage to the excellences to come.

And even more quickly riches became stale to him. And this time the fish came to his hand without even a net and ...

Note how we extend the fish metaphor even in the dialogue and in the process revivify delicately the cliche of 'small fry'. In the tank, Mr Higgins indulges himself with a somewhat jejeune symbol for market capitalism; presumably the lurking tentacle is a symbol for inflation, or something.

And what had seemed wealth to him came to seem each time the most abject poverty.

We had intended at this point to introduce the love interest, but Tony and Carol said that the public is not yet ready for threesomes with guppies. Instead, Mr Higgins steps into the breach with some neat chiaroscuro, and a piece of portraiture that for some reason makes our hero resemble a music-hall tutor.

In the Middle Ages, and in stories, you can't get away with that sort of thing, and the fish puts him back in Square, or rather Frame, One. Nowadays, wanting to be God is considered rather a modest aspiration; Mr Higgins and I are far more ambitious than that. Higgins of course insists on a neat ending, instead of the dying fall *I* planned, on a little ironic salt and vinegar for a character, who, as it were, has had his chips.

ENVY

TYM MANLEY and HUNT EMERSON

④

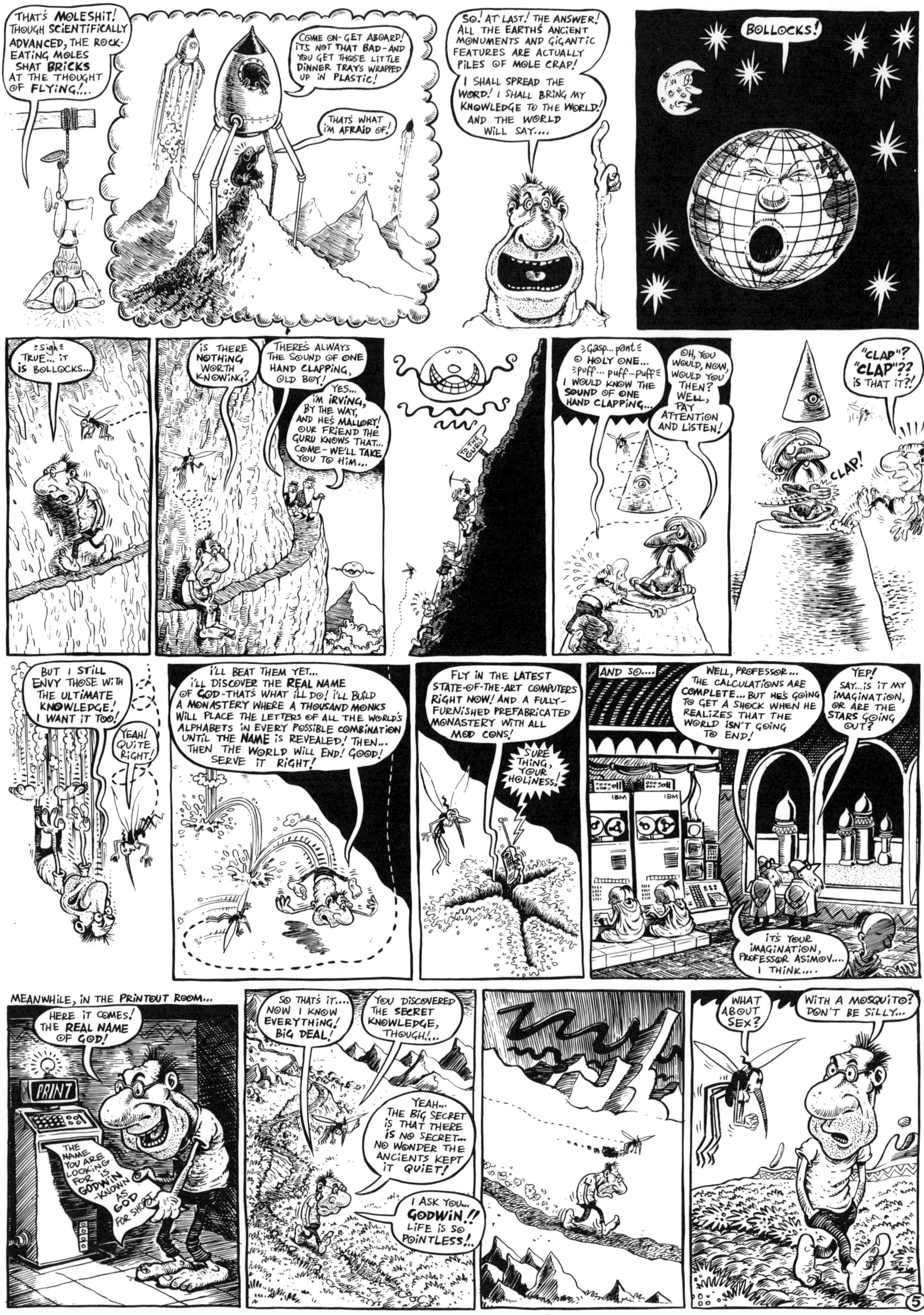

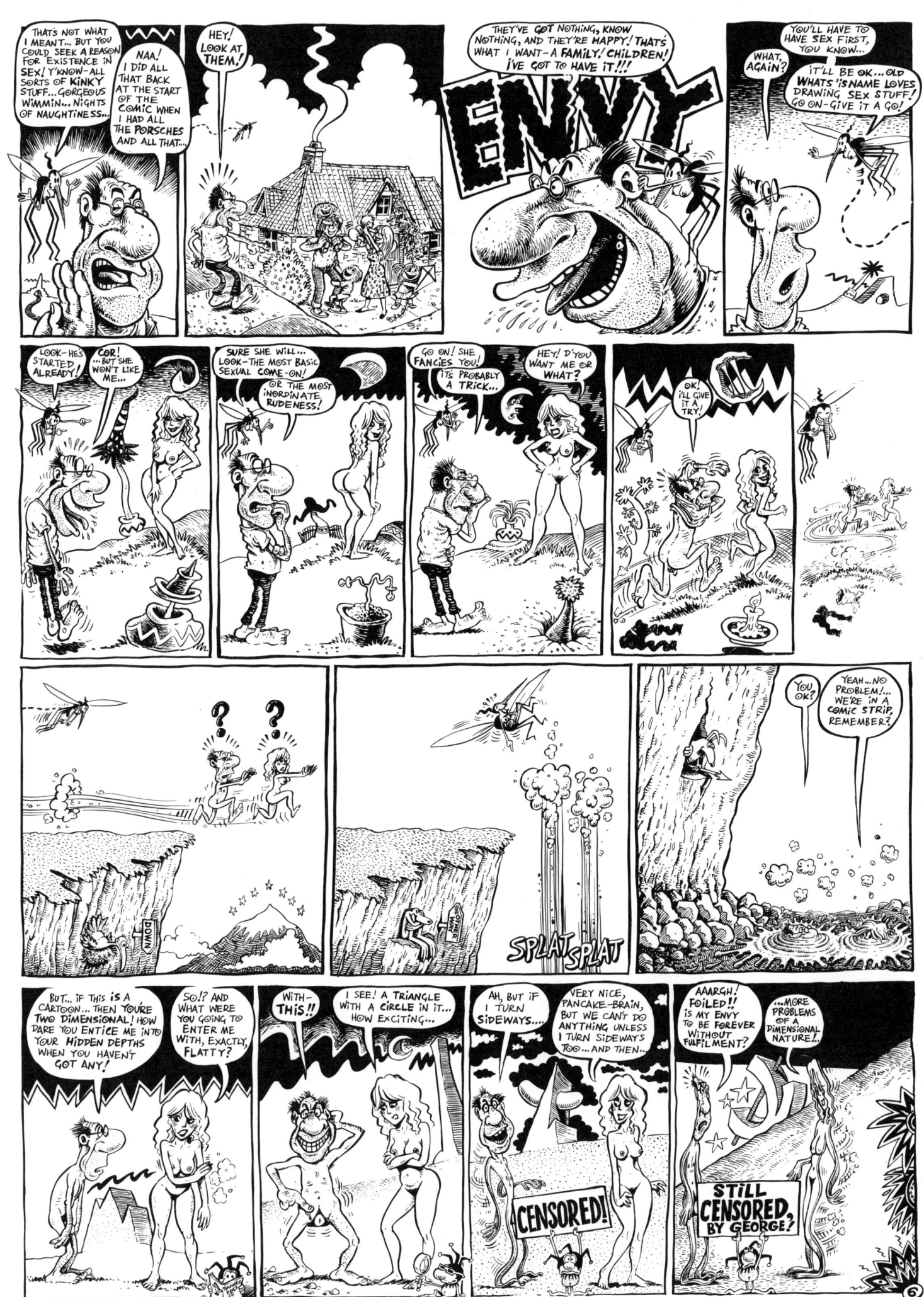

SLOTH

NEIL GAIMAN and BRYAN TALBOT

WE ARE THE FAMED LOAFING PILGRIMS OF HOVE, COME TO HEAR YOUR WORD, OH PROPHET. I AM **BROTHER TORPOR**, THIS IS **SISTER SLACK**, AND THAT IS **BROTHER SLUBBERDEGULLION**.

AND I'M NOT THE PROPHET. I AM BUT A MERE ACOLYTE.

THE PROPHET HIMSELF IS FAR TOO **HOLY** TO BE UP BEFORE LUNCH.

COME, THEN. LET US WAKE HIM, BROTHER TORPOR, SISTER SLACK AND BROTHER WITH A REALLY CRAP NAME.

IT'S SLUBBERDEGULLION. I DIDN'T BLOODY PICK IT.

IF IT'S WORTH HAVING IT'S WORTH WAITING FOR

TO WORK IS HUMAN TO RELAX DIVINE

All Comes To He Who

AWAKE, GREAT PROPHET! FOR AFTERNOON HATH COME UNTO THE WORLD ON THIS, THE FIRST DAY OF THE NEW MILLENNIUM! AND A BUNCH OF PILGRIMS ARE HERE TO DRINK YOUR WISDOM.

SOD OFF. CAN'T YOU SEE I'M ASLEEP, YOU USELESS WAZZOCK?

BLOODY HELL. ALL RIGHT. HAD TO GET UP EVENTUALLY.

YOU WANT TO KNOW HOW IT ALL HAPPENED, I SUPPOSE.

WELL, I WAS IN BED ONE MORNING, AND SUDDENLY I RECEIVED A VISION. SUDDENLY THREE GREAT MYSTERIES WERE REVEALLED TO ME.

TELL US ALL THREE OF THEM, GREAT PROPHET!

RIGHT.

WELL IN THE BEGINNING THE LORD **THOUGHT** ABOUT CREATING THE HEAVEN AND THE EARTH.

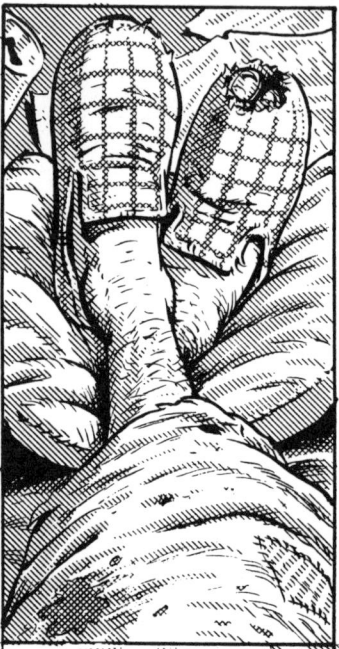

...And the Lord said unto Himself, Well, I've got all week, no need to hurry it. And truly He put His feet up.

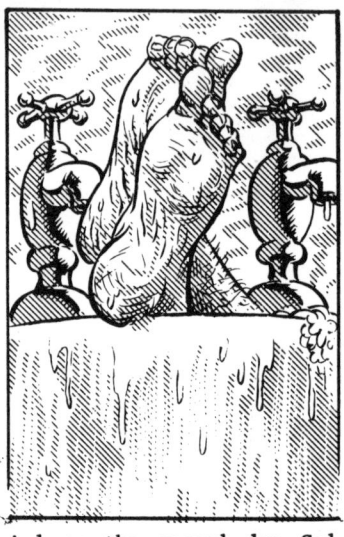

And on the second day God overslept. And then He created for Himself a nice hot bath, and some soap and a sponge and named He them, and the thriller to read in the bath created He, and it had the author's name embossed in large gold letters on the cover. And He saw it was good.

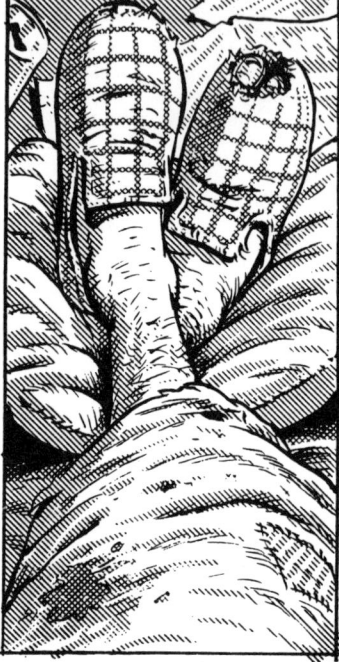

And that was half the day gone already, and He thought, Might as well start it tomorrow when I'm fresh.

And on the third day God rearranged His bookshelf. And people rang Him up and said unto Him, how's it going with the Heaven and Earth then? And He spake unto them, saying, almost finished, just a few details, be ready for Monday morning no problems.

And on the forth day He rested.

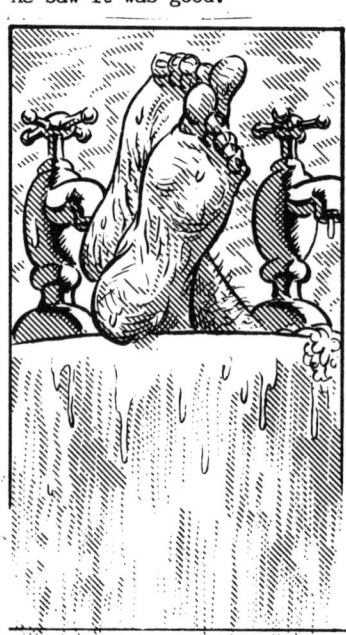

And on the fifth day He said Thank me, it's... um, I'll call it Friday, and it was Friday, which meant that it was coming up for the weekend, and He left early. And on Friday also did he have a bath.

And on the Saturday He walked around the house all day spaking unto himself, I've really got to get it done today. Honestly. Everybody's waiting. But He wasn't in the mood.

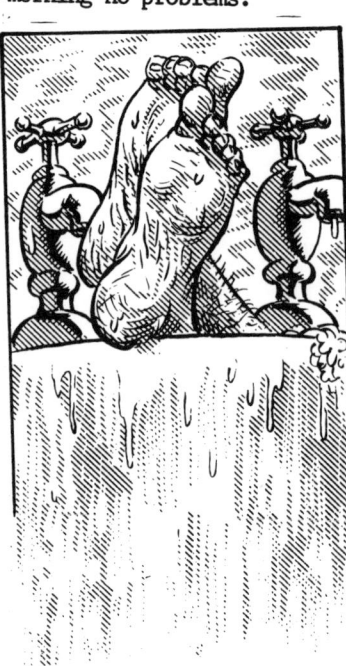

And on the Sunday he read the papers and had a late lunch and another bath. Also He trimmed the length of His Beard.

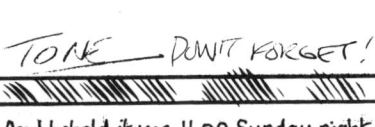

GLUTTONY

DAVE GIBBONS and LEW STRINGER

DO-GOODIN'? I COULD TELL YOU SOME STORIES ABOUT SO-CALLED DO-GOODIN'... F'RINSTANCE, TAKE THE 18TH AMENDMENT TO THE CONSTITUTION O'THIS HERE UNITED STATES. NOW, THAT WAS S'POSED TO DO *GOOD* WHEN THEY MADE IT *LAW*, BACK IN 1920. MOST FOLKS KNEW IT AS *PROHIBITION*...

FIDGET

FIDGET

GENERAL STORE

SCHOOL HOUSE

BARBER SHOP

IT *FORBAD* THE MAKIN' AND SELLIN' OF *LIQUOR*, THUS SAVIN' THE GREAT AMERICAN PUBLIC FROM THE EFFECTS OF DEMON *DRINK*.

SORRY FOLKS— NO BOOZE!

LEASTWAYS, THAT WAS THE IDEA THE *TEMPERANCE SOCIETIES* HAD, WHEN THEY FORCED THE LAW THROUGH *CONGRESS*.

DINGADI DINGADING!

POW!

REALITY WAS THAT *ORGANIZED CRIME* GOT A KING-SIZE *OPPORTUNITY* FOR *EXPANSION* HANDED TO IT ON A *PLATE*.

BARBER SHOP

SWIG!

THIS *HERE'S* A STORY 'BOUT DO-GOODIN' IN THEM PROHIBITION DAYS: IT CONCERNS *CRIME* AND *PUNISHMENT*, A SMALL-TOWN *TEMPERANCE SOCIETY* AND A MIGHTY INTEMPERATE MAN, *ALPHONSE GLUTTONE*, BETTER KNOWN ROUND THESE PARTS AS...

BARBERS

...THE GLUT!

AWFUL AFTER SHAVE AROMA

SPLOSH!

S'GOOD... GET MORE... ALL THEY GOT.

POP!

Y...!

HE'LL BE WANTIN' SOME *MORE* WHEN HE COMES FOR HIS SHAVE TOMORROW...

50 bottles Eureka After Shave

50 bottles Eureka After Shave

50 bottles

...AN' YOU BETTER *HAVE* SOME, IF YOU WANNA STAY ON THE RIGHT END OF YER *RAZOR!*

CERTAINLY GENTLEMEN. *ANYTHING TO OBLIGE!*

50 bo

SKREEE...

RRRRMMRR

SCRIPT: DAVE GIBBONS · ART: LEW STRINGER

THAT'S IT! THAT DOES IT! WE'VE HAD ENOUGH, HAVEN'T WE SARAH!?

Enough, Hanna.

THAT, THAT... PERSON THINKS HE CAN JUST COME TO THIS TOWN WITH ALL THE ILL-GOTTEN MONEY HE'S MADE FROM SELLING HIS EVIL LIQUOR AND JUST BUY ANYTHING HE WANTS AND BEHAVE HOW HE LIKES AND MAKE A LAUGHING STOCK OF THIS TOWN'S MOST RESPECTED CITIZENS, DOESN'T HE, SARAH?

...respected citizens, Hannah.

WELL, IF THE SO-CALLED MENFOLK OF THIS TOWN DAREN'T DO ANYTHING ABOUT IT, IT LOOKS LIKE IT'S UP TO YOU AND ME AGAIN, SISTER! AS SCHOOL PRINCIPAL AND CHAIRLADY OF THE TEMPERANCE SOCIETY, I PROPOSE WE MAKE AN OFFICIAL COMPLAINT TO THE FORCES OF LAW AND ORDER! AGREED, SARAH?

...forces of law and order, Hannah.

WE'LL SHOW THAT GANGSTER THAT WE'RE NOT INTIMIDATED BY HIS BULLY-BOY TACTICS! IF HE THINKS WE'RE THE KIND OF FOLK WHO RUN AND HIDE, HE'S GOT ANOTHER THINK COMING! HASN'T HE, SARAH?

...think coming, Hannah.

SCOOT!

NOW WHERE ON EARTH IS THAT MAN? IT'S NOT EVEN AS IF HE'S GOT ANYTHING TO DO AROUND HERE SINCE WE GOT ALL THE DRUNKENNESS STOPPED! YOU'D THINK HE'D BE GRATEFUL BUT ALL HE SEEMS TO DO IS AVOID US. ISN'T IT, SARAH?

...avoid us, Hannah.

SHERIFF! SHERIFF! SHERIFF!! SHERIFF!!

sheriff.

* HMnph. Wskyplz.

OH, er... MORNIN' LADIES. DROPPED M'BACCY. HOW KIN I HELP YOU TODAY?

IF YOU ASK ME, SHERIFF, YOU'D DO WELL TO DROP THAT TOBACCO OF YOURS PERMANENTLY! IN THE MEANTIME, WE WANT YOU TO DO SOMETHING ABOUT THAT DREADFUL GLUTTONE PERSON, DON'T WE, SARAH?

...permanently, Hannah.

YOU KNOW WHAT THAT GLUTTONE IS, DON'T YOU SHERIFF? A GANGSTER, THAT'S WHAT! AND YOU KNOW HOW HE MADE THAT MONEY HE THROWS AROUND, DON'T YOU? FROM CRIME, THAT'S WHAT! FROM BOOTLEGGING AND RUM-RUNNING AND FROM PROSTITUTION AND PORNOGRAPHY TOO, I WOULDN'T WONDER! AND NOW HE'S HERE IN OUR TOWN SETTING A TERRIBLE EXAMPLE TO OUR YOUNG FOLKS AND ENDANGERING EVERYONE'S MORALS AND WHAT WE WANT TO KNOW IS, SHERIFF, YOU'RE THE LAW IN THIS TOWN — WHAT DO YOU INTEND TO DO ABOUT IT?

* ahshtthfkupldy *

...prostitution and pornography.

WELL, LADIES...

...I DON'T RIGHTLY KNOW THERE'S ANYTHIN' I KIN DO! HE DON'T APPEAR TO BE BREAKIN' ANY LAWS THAT I KNOW OF.

BUT, AS IT HAPPENS, I GOT AN INVITE TO HIS PLACE TONIGHT FOR DINNER, SO I'LL SEE IF'N I KIN HAVE A NEIGHBOURLY WORD WITH HIM OVER THE SWEET POTATOES.

NEIGHBOURLY? DINNER?

sweet potatoes!

VERY WELL. COME ALONG, SARAH, WE HAVE LESSONS TO TEACH. JUST REMEMBER, SHERIFF, THAT WHEN ONE SUPS WITH THE DEVIL ONE SHOULD USE A LONG SPOON!

JAIL HOUSE

...long spoon, Hannah.

fkthdyl

ZZZZZZ

chugga chugga

CHUG CHU

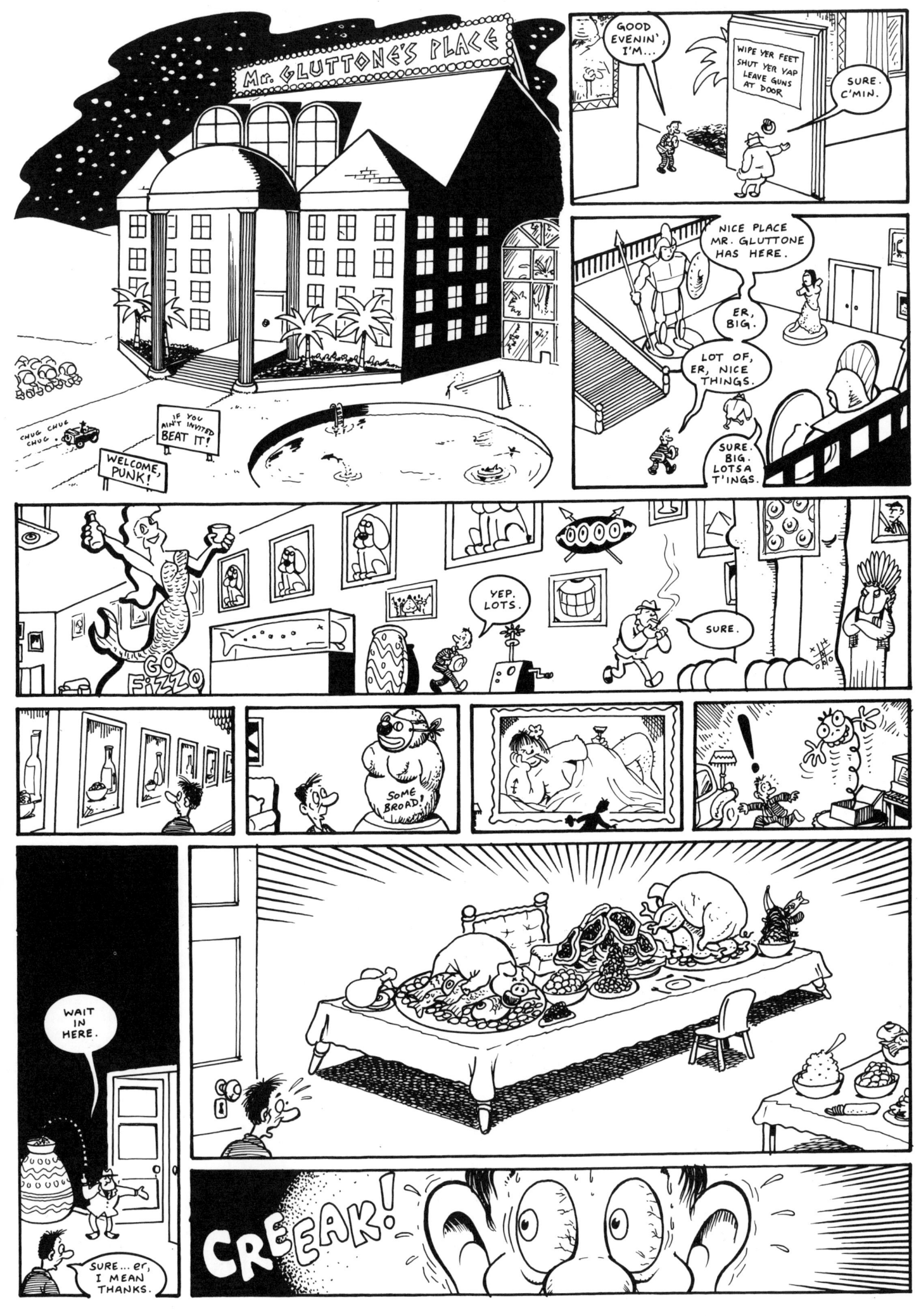

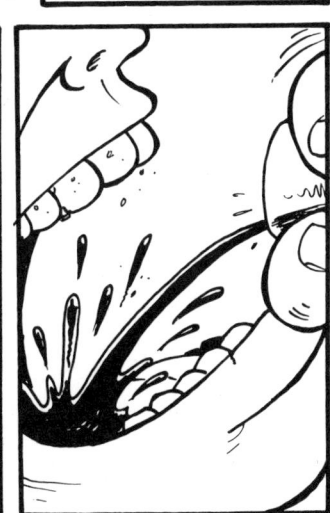

GUESS THAT'S THE PROBLEM WITH *DO-GOODIN'*: IT'S SO HARD TO BE SURE JUST WHAT'S *GOOD* AND WHAT'S *BAD*, IN THE LONG RUN. WHY, IN *CERTAIN* CIRCUMSTANCES, YOU MIGHT EVEN TURN A BLIND EYE TO *MURDER!*

ANYWAYS, *PROHIBITION* GOT REPEALED IN THE END, AND THE CITIZENS OF THE U.S.A. WERE ABLE TO BUY LIQUOR OVER THE COUNTER AGAIN, WHICH MADE EVERYONE HAPPY. 'CEPT THE *TEMPERANCE SOCIETIES*, THAT IS...

...AN', O'COURSE, THE *MOBSTERS.* BUT THEY SOON FOUND *OTHER* ILLEGAL DESIRES THAT NEEDED SATISFYIN' AN', WHAT WITH THE LESSONS THEY'D LEARNED, STARTED CATCHIN' CUSTOMERS EVEN *YOUNGER* AN' HOOKIN' 'EM ON EVEN *DEADLIER* STUFF.

YEP, CRIMES GOT EVEN *MORE* CUT-THROAT SINCE THOSE DAYS AN' JOHN Q. PUBLIC'S GOT *USED* TO LOOKIN' THE OTHER WAY. AS FOR DO-GOODIN', WELL, THE PUBLIC SORT'S *STILL* POPULAR BUT, LIKE ALWAYS, THE *REAL* THING GOES MORE OR LESS UNNOTICED.

FREE HAIRCUTS + SHAVE FOR WINOS + BUMS TODAY!

OH, *LOOK*, SARAH, *HERE* HE COMES *NOW!*

Now, Hannah.

GLUT-1

SOME *TURNOUT*, EH LADIES? RECKON HE'D HAVE *APPROVED.* MIND YOU, IT'S ALL FOR APPEARANCE SAKE. DOUBT HE HAD A *REAL* FRIEND IN THE WORLD...

THAT'S WHY WE HADDA CLOSE THE CASE. TOO MANY SUSPECTS.

HE TOOK A BIT O' *KILLIN'* TOO. HAD ENOUGH *RAT POISON* IN 'IM TO STOP AN *ARMY!*

JUST *LIKE* HIM, ALWAYS HAD TO HAVE A *BATH-TUB* FULL WHEN A *CUPFUL* WOULDA DONE ANY ORDIN'RY GUY.

SO WHO'DVE THOUGHT HIS WILL WOULD BE SO SHORT? "BURN EVERYTHING", THAT'S ALL IT SAID. "BURN EVERYTHING".

P'RAPS HE HAD A LOT OF *SECRETS*..

...OR PERHAPS HE LIKED TO IMAGINE *EVERYTHING* HE HAD BEING CONSUMED IN *ONE SITTING*, INSTEAD OF IN DRIBS AND DRABS. YEP, GUESS *THE GLUT* NEVER KNEW WHEN HE'D HAD *ENOUGH*...

...OR WHEN *PEOPLE* HAD HAD *ENOUGH* OF *HIM!*

Enough.

LEW STRINGER '89

THE BURRRPP! END!

GREED

MARK RODGERS and STEVE GIBSON

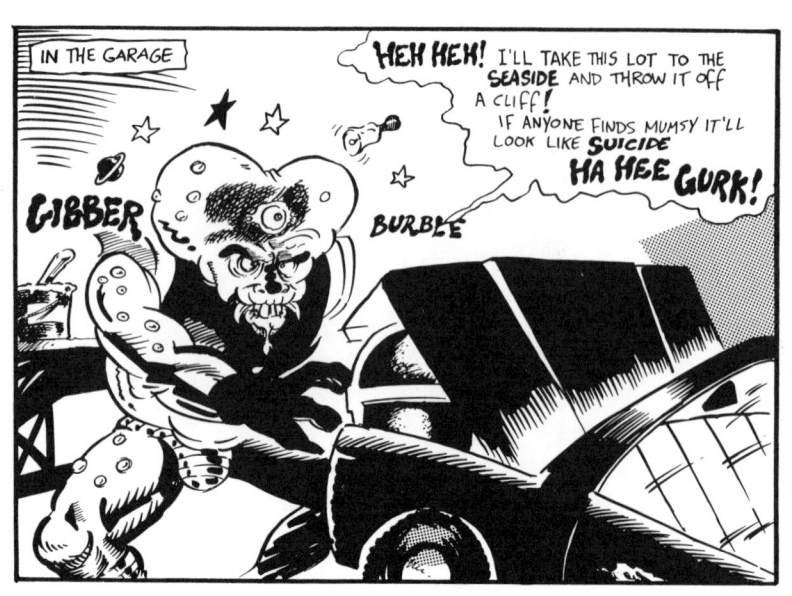

"HAVE IT ALL"
CAN'T SHAKE THEM OFF! THEY'RE CLOSING IN!!
SCREECH
CRIKEY! A VISION of HEAVEN!!!
GOLD AFTER SHAVE
Screw a different girl every night
VROOOM
SMASH!
AAAGH!
CRUNK
?
MOUNTAIN GOAT
BOOMF
CRUNCH!
SPRANG
Boi-oi-oing!
YEEOWCH!
HISS

THE LIVIN' END.

ANGER

DAVY FRANCIS and JEREMY BANKS

I REMAINED ANGRY IN SCHOOL...

...RIGHT THROUGH TO SECONDARY SCHOOL

I THAY, LETH GIVE THE NEW BOY A BATH

****

AS I HAD A FRAIL PHYSIQUE, I DECIDED TO DEVELOP MY BRAIN...

$E = MC^2$

AND I PASSED MY EXAMS WITH FLYING COLOURS...

CONGRATULATIONS MY BOY

THRRP

ALTHOUGH IT DID NOTHING TO LESSEN MY INNER BURNING...

I ENTERED THE WORLD OF INDUSTRIAL SCIENCE...

EUREKA! I'VE DEVELOPED A SUBSTANCE THAT CAN DISSOLVE ANYTHING

...BUT WITHOUT MUCH SUCCESS...

...AND I LEFT AFTER A DIFFERENCE OF OPINIONS...

GUARNIAD

LARGE HOLE IN AUSTRALIA DUE TO POWERFUL ACID

SOON AFTER, I ENTERED THE HELL-BLAZING WORLD OF ACCOUNTANCY...

...AND THIS IS MISTER FISK, HEAD OF THE SECTION

HALLO THERE - SO YOU'RE THE NEW BOY, ARE YOU?

A WORLD I FOUND TO BE TOTALLY FRUSTRATING

BIT OF AN ALBERT EINSTEIN, ARE YOU?

SCIENCE TODAY

FROM MORNING...

NO SMOKING

...'TIL NIGHT

OFF HOME ARE YOU?

NO- ACTUALLY, I'M WASHING A PELICAN'S BACKSIDE

DURING MY FREE TIME I BECAME A VIRTUAL RECLUSE. I WAS NEVER ASKED TO ANY OF MY NEIGHBOUR'S PARTIES...

I THINK MY NEIGHBOURS HATED ME AS MUCH AS I HATED THEM...

EVEN THE POSTMAN SENT ME HATE MAIL...

ONCE, I GOT A PET FOR COMPANIONSHIP...

HOWEVER THIS BOND DID NOT LAST LONG...

AND WE HAD TO PART OUR SEPERATE WAYS

I WENT ON A HOLIDAY TO TRY AND CALM MY NERVES — BUT EVEN THIS WAS INFURIATING...

AND WHEN I EVENTUALLY GOT TO MY DESTINATION, IT WAS EVEN WORSE...

EVEN SIMPLE THINGS MADE ME ANGRY - LIKE SHOPPING...

OR GOING TO THE BANK...

FINALLY, I RETIRED FROM MY "LIFE" IN ACCOUNTING...

WE KNEW YOU'D BE DRINKING LOTS OF CUPS OF TEA, SO WE GOT YOU THIS LOVELY KETTLE

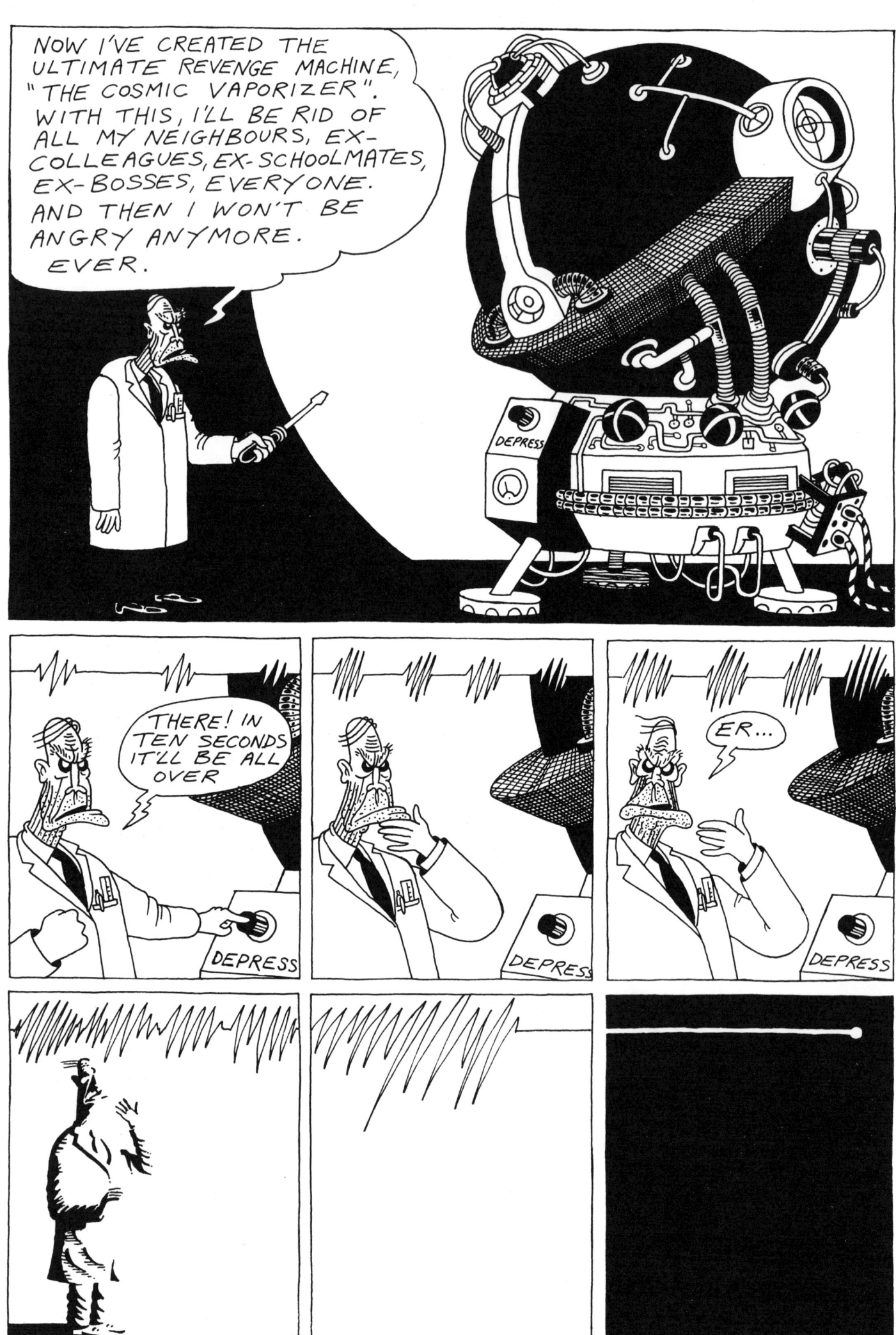

LUST

ALAN MOORE and MIKE MATTHEWS

LIVING JUST ACROSS THE WAY, WE'D BEEN WATCHING EACH OTHER FOR SOME TIME...

SHE HAD NICE CONTOURS, GOING IN AND OUT IN ALL THE RIGHT PLACES.

AND SHE WAS BUILT BIG..! THE WAY I LIKE 'EM.

SEEMS SHE HAD QUITE A REPUTATION.

BY ALL ACCOUNTS SHE'D SCREWED HALF OF EUROPE AND LEFT 'EM COMPLETELY IN HER THRALL..!

NOT THAT I WAS WORRIED... I'D SCREWED THE OTHER HALF, AND I HAD QUITE A REPUTATION MYSELF. I'VE GOT A BIG WEAPON THAT'S TALKED ABOUT FROM BIKINI RIGHT UP TO BERKSHIRE!

NO, SHE DIDN'T INTIMIDATE ME...

I LOOKED UPON HER AS...A CHALLENGE...!

LUST

A PORNOGRAPHY WRITTEN BY: ALAN MOORE ©'88 and ILLUSTRATED BY: MIKE MATTHEWS ©'88

COMING SOON!

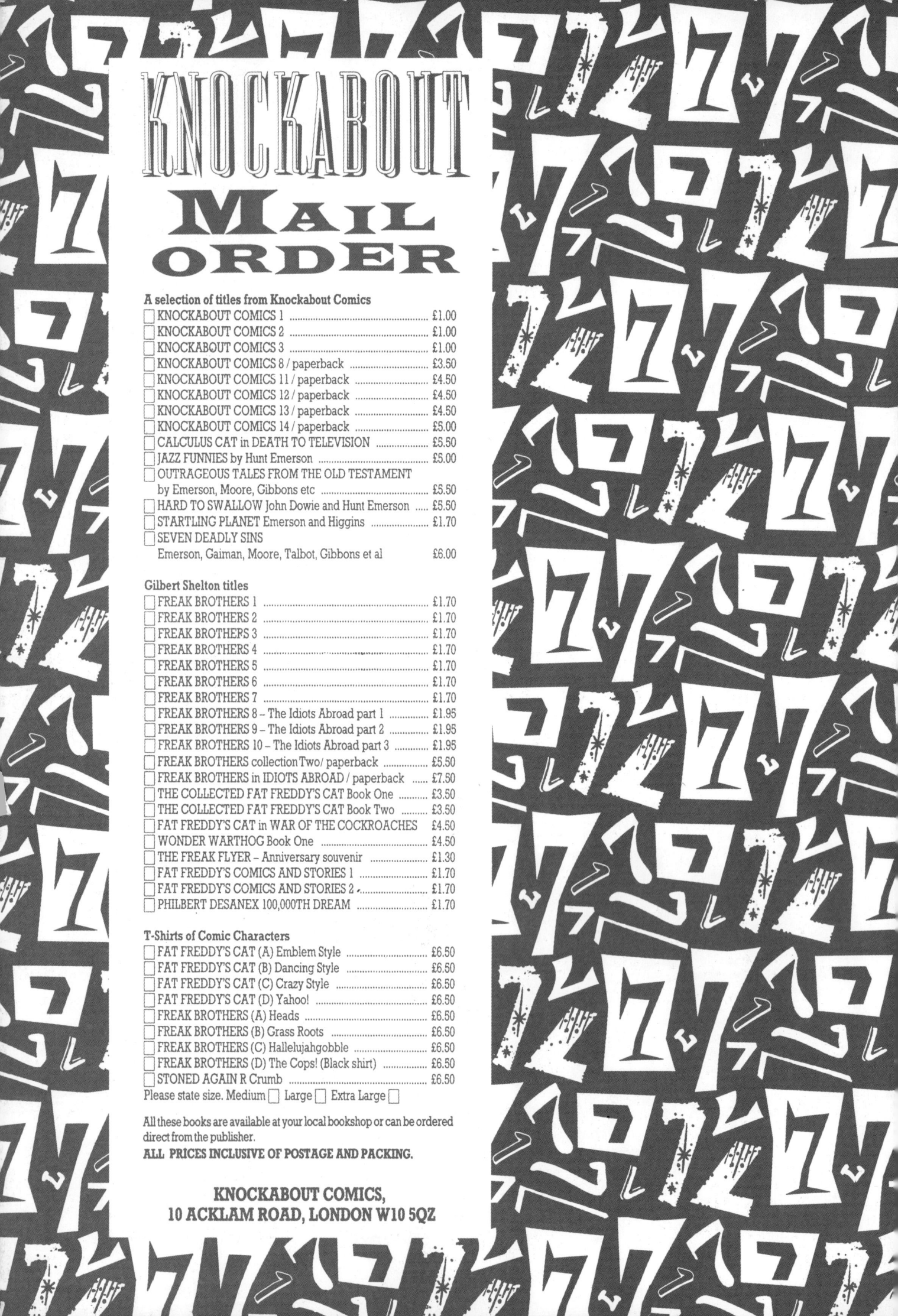

KNOCKABOUT
MAIL ORDER

A selection of titles from Knockabout Comics

☐ KNOCKABOUT COMICS 1 .... £1.00
☐ KNOCKABOUT COMICS 2 .... £1.00
☐ KNOCKABOUT COMICS 3 .... £1.00
☐ KNOCKABOUT COMICS 8 / paperback £3.50
☐ KNOCKABOUT COMICS 11 / paperback £4.50
☐ KNOCKABOUT COMICS 12 / paperback £4.50
☐ KNOCKABOUT COMICS 13 / paperback £4.50
☐ KNOCKABOUT COMICS 14 / paperback £5.00
☐ CALCULUS CAT in DEATH TO TELEVISION £5.50
☐ JAZZ FUNNIES by Hunt Emerson £5.00
☐ OUTRAGEOUS TALES FROM THE OLD TESTAMENT
   by Emerson, Moore, Gibbons etc £5.50
☐ HARD TO SWALLOW John Dowie and Hunt Emerson £5.50
☐ STARTLING PLANET Emerson and Higgins £1.70
☐ SEVEN DEADLY SINS
   Emerson, Gaiman, Moore, Talbot, Gibbons et al   £6.00

Gilbert Shelton titles

☐ FREAK BROTHERS 1 .... £1.70
☐ FREAK BROTHERS 2 .... £1.70
☐ FREAK BROTHERS 3 .... £1.70
☐ FREAK BROTHERS 4 .... £1.70
☐ FREAK BROTHERS 5 .... £1.70
☐ FREAK BROTHERS 6 .... £1.70
☐ FREAK BROTHERS 7 .... £1.70
☐ FREAK BROTHERS 8 – The Idiots Abroad part 1 ...... £1.95
☐ FREAK BROTHERS 9 – The Idiots Abroad part 2 ...... £1.95
☐ FREAK BROTHERS 10 – The Idiots Abroad part 3 .... £1.95
☐ FREAK BROTHERS collection Two/ paperback £5.50
☐ FREAK BROTHERS in IDIOTS ABROAD / paperback £7.50
☐ THE COLLECTED FAT FREDDY'S CAT Book One £3.50
☐ THE COLLECTED FAT FREDDY'S CAT Book Two £3.50
☐ FAT FREDDY'S CAT in WAR OF THE COCKROACHES £4.50
☐ WONDER WARTHOG Book One £4.50
☐ THE FREAK FLYER – Anniversary souvenir £1.30
☐ FAT FREDDY'S COMICS AND STORIES 1 .... £1.70
☐ FAT FREDDY'S COMICS AND STORIES 2 .... £1.70
☐ PHILBERT DESANEX 100,000TH DREAM £1.70

T-Shirts of Comic Characters

☐ FAT FREDDY'S CAT (A) Emblem Style £6.50
☐ FAT FREDDY'S CAT (B) Dancing Style £6.50
☐ FAT FREDDY'S CAT (C) Crazy Style £6.50
☐ FAT FREDDY'S CAT (D) Yahoo! £6.50
☐ FREAK BROTHERS (A) Heads £6.50
☐ FREAK BROTHERS (B) Grass Roots £6.50
☐ FREAK BROTHERS (C) Hallelujahgobble £6.50
☐ FREAK BROTHERS (D) The Cops! (Black shirt) £6.50
☐ STONED AGAIN R Crumb £6.50
Please state size. Medium ☐ Large ☐ Extra Large ☐

All these books are available at your local bookshop or can be ordered
direct from the publisher.
ALL PRICES INCLUSIVE OF POSTAGE AND PACKING.

**KNOCKABOUT COMICS,
10 ACKLAM ROAD, LONDON W10 5QZ**